Also by the author:

TWICE UPON A TIME, Moody Press
IN GOD'S HAND, Chalice Press
A FRESH WIND IN YOUR SAILS, West Bow Press
TO LOVE IN RETURN, West Bow Press

Clanging Halyards

Donald D. McCall

WESTBOW
PRESS®
A DIVISION OF THOMAS NELSON
& ZONDERVAN

WestBow Press books may be ordered through booksellers or by contacting:

WestBow Press
A Division of Thomas Nelson & Zondervan
1663 Liberty Drive
Bloomington, IN 47403
www.westbowpress.com
1 (866) 928-1240

[Scripture quotations are] from the New Revised Standard Version Bible, copyright © 1989 the Division of Christian Education of the National Council of the Churches of Christ in the United States of America. Used by permission. All rights reserved.

Scripture taken from the King James Version of the Bible.

ISBN: 978-1-9736-8406-0 (sc)
ISBN: 978-1-9736-8407-7 (hc)
ISBN: 978-1-9736-8405-3 (e)

Library of Congress Control Number: 2020901574

Print information available on the last page.

WestBow Press rev. date: 02/11/2020

Dedicated to my wife

Barbara Blazek McCall

"coniugi dilectissimae et amantissimae"

Contents

Acknowledgement

(She without whom none of these lines
would never have been written)

"You shall hear a whisper behind you, saying,
This is the way; walk in it."
Isaiah 30:21 KJV

Love lies not, as all fatalists think, in the luck of the draw,
Nor as the Predestined believe, in what they think they foresaw;
But rather, Love is in an inner voice that only the heart can hear
That comes when, as Isaiah proclaims, 'God whispers in your ear.'

For God in heaven has His own whisperers here on earth
Angels of Love who give human hearts a revivifying birth;
Whose love is the giving of one's self and all one's worth
To one's beloved... along with a mixture of madness and mirth

I must admit that at first, it was just once or twice
That I yielded to her better judgment and advice;
Then I learned that if it weren't for her encouragement
I never would have followed my heart's first intent
And my life would never have gone the way it went.

Why Use 'Clanging Halyards' for a Title

My son Donny...my namesake....my #1...called me from his lake home the other morning and said that the sound of the halyards clanging against the mainmast of his docked catamaran reminded him of all the great times we had sailing on lake Pepin in the years past and he just wanted to call and let me know that he missed me. I was in the early stages of writing my Fifth book and mentally searching for a title that would encompass all those same memories that generated my son's phone call to reminisce and remember those happy days in our lives. As we talked I thanked him for providing me with the title that i was looking for.

This book carries numerous Biblical texts alongside anecdotal accounts of the days of long ago alongside photographs of the days when the sun always shined and which many readers will remember, recognize or relate to as it reminds them of their own life experiences.

Surprisingly, it's a book of poetry. I guess I'm really an old romantic at heart.at least I hope so. I've chosen to entitle it: "Clanging Halyards" in recognition of son Donny's observation of looking back over all the memories that those clanging memories bring back to mind. Donny's phone call, which I'll always cherish, summarizes the full meaning of the consummation of my life.The memory of what is past is a continual joyful and daily reminder of the good times and the love of life and for each other that we have shared over the years. Now as I approach my 90th Birthday celebration I have another "to remember" moment to share with you: My Fifth Book !

I've enjoyed writing this book and I hope it will bring some of your old memories back to your mind as you read it.

PAX VOBISCUM

Preface

"You make us glad with the joy of your presence"
Psalm 21:6

It was dusk. Grandson Jordan would be home from school shortly. He had been with us for over ten years.

Shortly after his mother and father had both graduated from the University Of Nebraska College Of Medicine and were preparing for their year-long Residency in Madison, Wisconsin. David's sister Jen was a young attorney in Madison. David's older sister, Betsy was also a young attorney in Madison so Barbara and I decided to sell our home in Lincoln Nebraska and move to Madison to assist David and Jameca raise their baby Jordan. It was one of the best decisions we ever made! We all landed in the same large apartment complex across the street from the University of Wisconsin college of Medicine. Barb and I had a 3-bedroom apartment on the 3rd floor directly above David and Jameca's 3-bedroom apartment on the first floor. I would say that it was a 'divinely ordained' situation. Barb says we moved from our 'haven' in Lincoln to 'a bit of heaven' in Madison.

For over ten years Jordan was the loving nester that brought us all together....as well as the occasion now for the writing of this book.

When Jordan ran into our apartment that afternoon, he couldn't wait to show me an award he won at school for poetry. I hugged him and congratulated him (a combination of events I was getting used to) and then said in surprise, "Poetry?" I was used to congratulating him for bringing home sports trophies. But poetry? We talked about the intimacy of poetry...the delicacy of its language...the depth of its feelings; then I confessed to him that I often wrote poems and even had some of them published. I pulled an old briefcase out from a file cabinet and we looked at some of my published poems. Then, having just finished writing my fourth book, I promised that I'd write one for him .... a book of poetry: and here it is !

Destiny

A poem I wrote at 18 yrs. of age while serving on the Pacific Ocean on board the Navy Destroyer USS Brush DD 745 during the Korean War.

Psalm 118:22. and Matthew 21:42
"The stone the builders rejected has become the chief cornerstone"

DESTINY

The mason cast THE STONE aside
To fall afoot the passing tide

Of human's hurried building pace.
And soon the stone had lost its place
In man's designs and building space
The building was finished
And all stones were in station;
All save one for the corner location
Workmen looked and searched the land
And found THE STONE in the dusty sand
Once cast aside... now placed in honored stand!

So, if O Lord I seem to be
Overlooked in my locality,
Let me work and strive and pray to be
Ready for my destiny...

Two Sailors with the Same Visions and Dreams

"Your young men will see visions; your old men will dream dreams."Acts 2:17

Saturday:

We drove to the marina sharing the same purpose and intent,
To buy a sailboat, as if we were on a mission that was heaven sent;
My grandson peeking through a porthole to check the cabin's vent
Then relaying what he saw to Grandpa whose
aged body was hobbled and bent.

What my grandson observed, and what he excitedly related to me,
With the sound of the clanging halyards,
reinforcing my aged memory;
Seeing that his youthful vision and my old
man's dreams merged momentarily
And I realized that the pleasure of his presence
was ordained providentially!

I've often wondered what this verse in the book of Acts meant,
And now I understand and am able to move on quite content,
Knowing that this old sailor's life has been well spent
Having bonded with my grandson as we
shared the same purpose and intent.

Thoughts After a Brief Morning Spat

"The wolf shall dwell with the lamb and the
leopard shall lie down with the kid,
And the calf and the lion and the fatling together...
And the suckling child shall play over the hole of the asp...
They shall not hurt or destroy in all my mountain ..."
Isaiah 11:6-9

Forget the wolf and the lamb lying down, side by side
I'd be more content with a minor little miracle;
Perhaps one not unlike what the prophet decried,
Yet one that doesn't sound so profoundly Biblical

I'm more concerned about our life here on the prairie
About our daily silly little flares of ego and tempers;
Whereby we hurt and destroy each other unnecessarily
Through our bumbling blunders in our daily encounters

So, forget the wolf and the lamb and the suckling child,
For the real test in life for us on earth is this...
To lie down together at each days-end .... Reconciled
While learning to live together in peaceful bliss!!

Sloth

*Through sloth the roof sinks in… and through indolence
the building leaks" Ecclesiastes 10:18*

Ah, Sloth, I know thee all too well
Thou and indolence thy linguistic twin:
For as Scripture does so clearly foretell
Thou art the cause of my roof falling in !

Inertia is your instant inclination
Which prompts me toward further procrastination;
And though I wish there were some other explanation
Thou hast become the cause of my barn's dilapidation!

Well, I hope to fix the roof... someday soon
But getting started is what's so very hard;
Maybe I'll put it off until tomorrow afternoon
After I get an estimate from the lumber yard!

So once again SLOTH you've done me in
You and your twin indolence are going to win;
Whispering in my ear that this may not be the best time to begin
And causing me to become complicit in my own barn's ruin!

Remembering Our Roots

(Celebrating the 500th Anniversary of the Reformation)

John 17:21

We were all One … Once.

Luther, Calvin, Zwingli and Knox

Scholar-preachers whose hermeneutical response

Created a new and confounding doctrinal paradox.

We called it the Reformation.
Its roots were deeply entwined in Gospel texts;
Its Thesis nailed to the Wittenberg Church door as a declaration
Of all matters of faith and practice in this world and the next.

We cherished our new polity,
We captured and codified its thinking in our theological creeds
Establishing new denominations from city
to city, from century to century
Tailoring the truth of that seamless robe to meet our cultural needs.

We branched out in different directions so much
And grew equally so distant from one another;
That now our branches barely touch
And our leaves barely know each other.

It looks to me now as if we are about to split and fall
I see no way to bring our boughs once again together:
Yet in my heart I wish we could somehow change it all
And fulfill the desire of Jesus in His Gethsemane prayer:
"I ask only that those who believe in me may all be one"

Crossing the River Styx

Colossians 1:13

In ancient history the Greek philosophers had an elaborate system which allowed the Soul of the departed to find its way into the afterworld. They believed that the god Hermes would assist you and act as your host at the approaching time of your death. Hermes would lead you to the shore of the mythical River Styx to reach the afterlife. Furthermore, they believed that a ferryman named Charon would give you a ride (for a fee) on his boat. Thus it is that 'dying' is still often referred to as 'crossing the River Styx.'

I was beginning to sense my own death in the very near distance,
While at the same time, I dreaded the thought of my own demise;
My heart recoiled in apprehensive fear and mortal resistance;
While I asked myself "Is this what happens when one dies?"

Soon I felt the arm of my youngest son's loving embrace
As he gently led me down to the broad Rivers edge;
I prayed for deliverance through God's redeeming Grace
As I stood there trembling at the shore's well-worn ledge.

My older son stood waiting on his boat … moored at its slip,
And loving son that he is, he welcomed me aboard;
And then ferried me across the river on a final languishing trip
Where on the other side I was "Transferred
to the Kingdom" of my Lord.

The Sahara of the Soul

*A scribbled note from the journal I kept while
motorcycling across the Sahara Desert*

The desert transforms itself ... by itself, every night
Through shifting winds and sifting sands;
Then it wakens anew at dawn's earliest light,
To face whatever challenge a new day demands.

That's the transformation I was seeking in my spiritual life,
While sifting through all it was that my heart was feeling;
Trying to sense the shifting winds in life's stormy strife
That winnows the spirit from the chaff in all my being.

However, the answer I found was not the answer I sought
Nor was it one of great theological profundity;
T'was a prayer in a book that I packed as an afterthought
Written by St. Augustine during his transforming journey:

"O Lord, my God, behold and see and have mercy and heal me,
Thou in whose presence I have become a problem to myself;
and that is my infirmity (1)

I instantly knelt down and offered that prayer so long overdue
Using my motorcycle as my own prie-dieu
I confessed that infirmity which I had long known to be true:
That I was the problem that needed to be transformed anew.

** *(1) Confession of St. Augustine, E.P.. Dutton NY, NY pg 151*

They Roofed Her Once Too Often

Psalm 38:4-22

"For my iniquities have gone over my head, they weigh like a burden too heavy for me... For I am ready to fall... I confess my iniquity. I am sorry for my sin. Do not forsake me, O Lord, make haste to help me!"

They roofed her once too often,
This old barn, now long neglected;
Her broken beams so weather beaten
Make me doubt she'll ever be resurrected!

The tragedy lies, as you might surmise
In that her collapse was not from neglect;
For she was the cause of her own demise
In wanting to cover what she wanted to protect!

Her constant re-covering was her own undoing.
For as each new roof was added and applied,
The mounting burden of weight accruing
Caused her to collapse... from the inside.

I sometimes sense I'm collapsing from within,
not from life's burdens upon me spread;
But from continually recovering every little sin
until it weighs 'like a burden over my head'.

A Beggar in Rajipur

(A poem I wrote while I was hiking up the Himalayas in India)

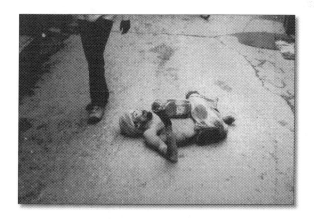

Matthew 25:40

This beggar lying in the marketplace of old Ragipur
One among thousands of India's homeless poor,
Cried out to me with pleas of dire distress
Begging for alms to ease his helplessness;
Looking at me with hope that only Love understands
As if to say that his life was in my hands!

Then slowly the beggar inched away
Without the coins he hoped I'd cast his way;
And in my heart I heard the words I'd heard so often:
"Inasmuch as you do it unto the least of these, my Brethren"
And I knew then that Judgment lies in what love demands,
And that it was my life that was in the beggars hands!

A Communion Prayer

Psalm 91:4
*"He will cover you with His pinions,
And under his wings you will find refuge."*

I'm old. I'm very old. This is my 90th year on Planet Earth
Serving as a pastor, preacher and Homiletics Professor;
And today, is the first day since the day of my birth
That I've experienced "LOVE" as I've never known it before;

It was after Holy Communion and the singing of a hymn
That while I was placing my cup in one of the pew cup holders,
I suddenly felt the touch of the wings of a heavenly Seraphim
Brush against my body and come to rest upon my shoulders.

And I knew that God was nigh and making His presence known
Covering me with His pinions as a sign of heavenly affirmation
Of that LOVE which claims to bless it's beloved as its own;
LOVE which I still felt… until we rose for the benediction
And my Granddaughter let her arm fall from my shoulders !

Minister Appreciation Month

We once had a minister whom I truly detested
Whose preaching was perhaps his very worst fault;
In fact, I thought he should have been arrested
And charged with several counts of verbal assault!

He called us names, like "unrepentant sinners"
And once even said we were like "a brood of vipers"
We often saw him eating and drinking at public dinners
With unclean people like tax collectors and hucksters.

But now we have a minister whom I really admire
Whose sermons are always humorous and brief;
And although we know he's "preaching to the choir"
It has been for us, something of a relief!!!

He tells us that God loves us ever so dearly
That it really doesn't matter what we do or say;
And he says it so convincingly and so sincerely
That I no longer even feel the need to pray!

So tell me now, why is my soul so ill at ease
And why does my mind still wonder and doubt;
And why does my heart have no sense of peace
And why do I feel less fervent and devout???

I think I'd like my old minister back
For now, I've come to realize and sense,
That he was probably right on track
And I was the one so dumb and dense
As to take umbrage and personal offense
At the Gospel's attack against my indifference
And my spiritual and moral indolence!!!

DONALD D. MCCALL is honorably retired
and lives in Madison, Wisc.
The Presbyterian Outlook a September 21/28, 2009

Love Never Ends

I Corinthians 13:8
"Love believes all things... hopes all things. Love never ends"

My two daughters standing and staring out into the sea
Watching over my two grandsons wading out into the surf;
Reawakens all those old memories, so precious to me
Of what's important in life and what's of eternal worth!!!

I remember the days long ago when I stood on the shore
And watched as they waded forth to face life on their own;
And now as I age and realize I'm approaching death's door
My happiest thoughts are to see how loving they have grown!

I know what my two daughters are thinking and feeling
as they watch my two grandsons challenge the waves
And now I hope they have faith enough to risk believing
That Love will also guide them through all their days.

I see now that my life's greatest joy and achievement
Has not been any accomplishment or doing of my own;
But rather it lies in seeing the fruits of love's fulfillment
Carried on in the love that my children have shown!!!

Who Is My Neighbor?

And a Lawyer asked Jesus, "Who is my neighbor?"
Luke 10:29

When I was chairing the Nebraska State Board of Parole
I held a weekly closed door meeting for all the new convicts;
Murderers, rapists, arsonists and those who robbed and stole,
Those whose crimes were either active or complicit.

I was there alone to help them cope with their new condition
To warn them of the danger of receiving a violation citation;
To answer any questions they had about their incarceration
And the importance of avoiding any disciplinary notations

Recently, after a weekly offender's closed door meeting
I received a letter thanking me for offering 'closed door' groups.
My former lawyer/neighbor then concluded with this final greeting;
"I do miss walking by your house and seeing the kids shooting hoops."

I hadn't even recognized my own now incarcerated neighbor!
(Frankly, in prison garb everyone looks the same.)
I began to realize that I was the one the parable was written for
And my embarrassment reflected my own sense of shame.

I've thought about that letter…ever since
He was a lawyer who knew who his neighbor was;
I was the one Jesus was trying to convince
To be equally magnanimous.
(I'm trying to)

The Best Medicine

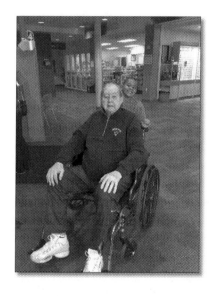

"A cheerful heart is the best medicine!"
Proverbs 17:2

How True!How True!
Grandson Jordan is taking me where I do not want to go.
He does it because he knows it's what he has to do…
And so, he obliges with a smile and a face aglow!

What he doesn't know is that his smile is the world's best medicine
Scripture records that it's the healing power
for every old and weary soul....
And if you look closely you can see the healing starting to begin
And Grandpa's smile in return is beginning to show!

"I tell you, when you were younger you used to fasten your own belt and go wherever you wished, But when you grow old, someone else will fashion a belt around you and take you where you do not wish to go." John 21:18

My First Car

My first car was this 1926 Model T Ford
A $20 bargain I could easily afford;
This photo captures the memory of that moment not to be missed.
A moment of teenage elation like the memory of life's first kiss!

Some 'firsts' in life are never to be forgotten
They're too precious to be relegated to "way back when"
Like this picture of me at sixteen, sharing a moment of ecstatic Zen
While tinkering with my car's engine, over and over again

My first car, like my first Love
Will forever have a special place in my heart…
Especially the remembrance of needing a
few friends to give her a shove
Or to crank her long enough to get her to start!

My wife tells me that at my age
I'm kind of the same way too:
She says that sometimes I'm like a wild tiger pacing in his cage
But more often out of commission, while
awaiting a new part or two!

On Love and Marriage

"Therefore, a man cleaves to his wife, and they become one flesh."Genesis 2:24

I was brushing my teeth early this morning
And I glanced down and was surprised to see,
That just between the two of us, my Darling
We have five toothbrushes, all of equal quality!

Granted:
We drink from the same cup
We eat off the same plate;
And we don't have any hang-up
As to how we osculate!

So, why five toothbrushes in the cup?
I guess it's one of the mysteries of marriage;
Not your first thought when you wake up,
But one of the things you ponder at my age!

But what really got my attention this morning
Was that the brush of my own choosing?
Was already wet, which should have been a warning
That it was the same one that you've been using!

Now I understand what God said about Adam and Eve
That "the two shall become one flesh"
But for the life of me, I find it hard to believe
That God said, "And they shall both use one brush"

A Spider's Web

Psalm 9:16 "The wicked are snared in the work of their own hands"

In the back of my mind, I have a hunch,
That this spider is patiently waiting for his lunch,
Hoping to entrap or cleverly ensnare
Some unsuspecting insect flying through the air.

But I can see his web, and he can't fool me
I'll easily circumvent his ingenuity;
So… why can't I see the countless snares
That always seem to trap me unawares?
I think this spider has taught me a lesson,
For now I can see that in my every transgression,
And that in all the temptations around me rising
I am simply being ensnared in the webs of my own devising!!!

Sitting in My Backyard by the Pool

Vis –a- Vis

SITTING BY THE POOL AT BETHESDA

John 5:6

I was sitting in my backyard, relaxing by our swimming pool
With my dog at my side where it was shady and cool:
When I was suddenly surprised to hear the Master's voice
Propounding a question wherein he offered me a simple choice:
"Do you want to be healed?" *

It was the very same question I suddenly realized
That he asked a crippled man who for 38 years sat paralyzed
Waiting for the "stirring of the waters" by the pool of Bethesda
Unaware that his was not a physical but a Spiritual miasma.
"Do you want to be healed?"

It's a question that seems at first to be a bit absurd
He had spent his life sitting by the pool hoping to be cured;
But it had become such a comfortable way of living
That he had completely forgotten his earlier dreams for healing.
"Do you want to be healed?"

Jesus knew that my problem was my unwillingness to disown
The lifestyle that kept me ensconced in my own comfort zone.
I wasn't pursuing the 'High Calling' I vowed 38 years ago
Instead I'd grown accustomed to the comforts of the status quo !
Alas Lord… Forgive me …

I should have been stirring up the waters
Or at least stirring up the hearts of others;
And now, to answer your question, I'm appealing
For your forgiveness and restorative healing.

A Quiet Place

Mark 6:31 "Come ye apart to a quiet place and get some rest."

I stop here at my son's home at least twice a year,
To rest, recover and see who I really am;
It's a place where I welcome God to interfere
As a shepherd would with a wayward lamb.

Here it is that "all nature rings and round me sings"
And reminds me of the path I've been called to travel;
Here it is that my conscience renews all those things
That time allows itself to forget or unravel.

It's being here in this place that renews my power and energy
It's also my son's home and his earthly domain;
Which also represents all that he is and has come to be...
And I'm beginning to wonder if he is living
the life I once sought to attain!

God's Prevenient Grace

"Thou preventest me with blessings of goodness" Psalm 21:3 KJV

Somehow, as I look at this old fence
I begin to realize and slowly sense
That it symbolically represents
God's loving care and omnipresence.

Its rail are still both strong and stout:
And as I stand and look all roundabout
It causes me to wonder and to doubt
That it was ever made to keep ME out.

Rather than being built to keep, me away
I believe it was placed there more to hedge my path;
Lest at times I might wander and stray
And thus incur God's righteous wrath!

So it is in life that I'm often thus prevented
From doing what my foolish heart intended;
And my plans were thus circumvented
And I think I now have finally comprehended:

'Twas God's prevenient grace that hedged me in
And kept my soul thus free from sin!

The Three Amigos

Matthew chapters: 5, 17, and 26

There are several times in the Gospels (Matthew 5, 17, and 26) when Jesus takes three of his disciples (Peter, James and John) aside from the others in order to share a private moment with them. It is not an uncommon practice for teachers, mentors and sojourners even to this day. Sometimes such a meeting is fortuitously totally accidental.

Here are three of my grandchildren who surprisingly met
At O'Hare's overly congested airport in Chicago;
While their families were traveling in different directions,
And their flights all made various untimely connections.

It reminded me of the Three Musketeers by Alexandre Dumas;
Athos, Parthos and Aramis; inseparable in all their adventures;
Whose motto was "All for one, and one for all one has"
And the power that Friendship generates in cousin's coeurs.

I was glad to see that my three grandchildren
Have intuitively developed that quality of friendship
That will continually enhance their lives even when
That continuity finds its basis in kinship!

Training a Child

Proverbs 22:6 KJV
"Train a child in the way she should go and she will
never depart from it"

I love training Karen in the way a golf ball should go,
And watching it zoom straight down the open fairway;
For if there's one thing I've learned …or one thing I know
It's that helping her helps me each time we pley!

The fact is that this text is more than about one thing;
The greater truth that scripture seems to imply;
Is that while she's mentally grooving her swing
I'm at the same time improving mine…or at least I try.

Sanctus Benedictus

(An old man's thought during Holy Communion)

I came home last week from the Doctor's office
Where he confirmed again and earlier diagnosis;
Which added more meds for my prostate and Diabetes
Along with high blood pressure and a possible prosthesis;
And now I'm told that according to the latest analysis
Alzheimer's will soon leave me 'non compos mentis'.
So...
My endocrinologist has put me on Diabetic medication,
My audiologist has suggested a cochlear implantation,
My optometrist is checking for macular degeneration,
My internist wants a through memory evaluation,
My proctologist fills me with fear and trepidation
And my dermatologist wants to do skin rejuvenation,
But...
I want nothing to do with any of it
For I sense myself to be perfectly fit
For this morning in church where I usually sit
I didn't feel myself to be that totally decrepit:

And when the minister rose to speak from the pulpit
I was overcome by the healing power of the Heavenly Spirit...
For...
I heard every word of the minister's homily
And every syllable of the ancient liturgy;
Perhaps not exactly as it was spoken audibly
But at least as the Holy Spirit interpreted to me...
And...I saw in my mind's eye ever so clearly
All the faces of those whom I love so dearly
Gathered around the Table there to share with me
The loaf and the cup in quiet sanctity.
Then...
As we sang those great hymns of faith and love
My memory took wing like that of a heavenly dove
And my mind was quickly awakened with memories of
All the yesterdays of my life and all the joys thereof!
And...
As our prayers to heaven did ascend
And the benediction of peace upon us descend;
I suddenly realized, and slowly began to apprehend
That even my heart had been renewed by morning's end.
So, Thank You, Lord for the healing power
Of this morning's Worship Hour.

Sursum Corda

Matthew 23:25

When the minister invited us to lift up our hearts in prayer
My wife slipped her hand into mine in tender loving care;
It's a moment each week during the service of worship
When we clasp our hands together in love's embracing grip.

However, this week I did happen to notice something new,
For as she placed her right hand in mine, I caught in full view...
Her left hand doing something I could hardly believe.
She was deftly lifting up lint from my sport coat's sleeve.

Theologically, I would say that she was "cleansing me from lint"
Which actually should have been an obvious homiletical hint;
That it's not what's on the outside of the sleeve or the cup
But the inside of my errant heart that needed a bit of cleaning up!

But to tell the truth ... I rather appreciated her loving attention,
For I do enjoy being cared for with such tender loving affection;
And frankly, during long prayers

I don't think God really cares,
In the course of human affairs
Whether we're lifting up our hearts or lifting up lint
As long as we let Love express its own momentary stint.

Thoughts on a College Graduate
Who Still Lives at Home

I have a tree whose leaves won't leave
Though winter winds blow blizzard gales
But still my leaves securely cleave
And stubbornness prevails
I think I understand those leaves
For we have a son who's just like that
And yet no matter what his mother believes
I think it's time for him to scat!

A Realm Too Deep for Human Thought

The Doctrine of Election

The Bible is emphatic that the choice is with God, rather than
with man. This is the basis of the Biblical Doctrine of Election.
The Old Testament writers could never understand the reason
for this choice and content themselves with the statement of the
fact of the choice. St. Paul similarly concludes: "Oh the depth
of the...wisdom and the knowledge of God! How unsearchable
are His judgments and inscrutable his ways." Romans 11:33

John 15:16 "Ye have not chosen me, but I have chosen you"

I put out food to entice
Both the squirrels and the mice;
Both wee rodents need me for their survival
And I each day solicit their arrival;

Setting out food that that's fit for a king
And a feast that catered to their individual liking!
Peanut butter for the squirrel and cheese for the mice;
As if they were at a banquet in paradise!

But now, the problem arises
And I'd like to know what your advice is:
What part of me then becomes so divisive?
That I should save the squirrels and then kill the mices?

The Last Robin of Summer

The Last Robin of summer stopped by this afternoon
And paused on the stone wall of my backyard;
Making one last visit, knowing that all too soon
It would be time for him to start flying southward!

He sat there looking south for the longest while
As if he were debating in his little bird mind,
Whether or not wintering at some sea swept isle
Would be better than what he was leaving behind!

I'd like to believe that he enjoyed nesting here
That he loved my leafy trees and wormy sod;
And knowing that I was always present and near
Was to him like living in the presence of God!

But I know him to be a creature of habit
A migratory bird that knows its seasons;
Whose brief and pleasant summertime visit
Ends simply because of Darwinian reasons

Sometimes I wish that I had his good sense
And that I could fly south to some warm winter place!
But I think that for me what makes all the difference
Lies in the fact that I have a monthly mortgage to face!

Que Sera, Sera

"Search me, O God and know my heart
Test me and know my thoughts" Psalm 139:23

Granddaughter Ava looking out to sea
Wondering about her future destiny;
Developing her life's philosophy;
And whatever her future may be.

Fatalism, Determinism, Atheism
Empiricism, Rationalism, Scholasticism,
Or as the songster suggests in our modern era
In the philosophy of "QUE SERA SERA"!

But my thought for someone of your age
Is to first seek out more in life than mere knowledge;
I'd begin with the dictum, "Know Thyself First"
And in that search be immersed!

Note:
John Calvin in his monumental work "Institutes of Christian Religion" states in his opening pages that all wisdom consists of coming to know God and that it is in knowing God that one comes to know oneself. Calvin was right and his insight is still applicable for us today.

Amazing Grace

Deuteronomy 22:6

I came upon this bird's nest quite by chance
As I was trimming a rosebush in my backyard;
I was a little taken aback at first glance
By a moral dilemma that caught me off guard.

Should I take the eggs and leave the nest
Or leave the eggs and hope for the best;
Or is my dilemma simply an ethical test
Wherein the issue of Salvation is addressed?

Then it came to me in a moment of awe,
That for every such unusual circumstance
There was written instruction in OT law
Wherein I would find words of God's guidance!

And so I searched the Book of Deuteronomy
For instruction regarding the wee eggs salvation;
And what I discovered was distressing to me
For the Law commanded their eradication!

"If you chance to come upon a bird's nest,
Either in a tree or on the ground...
You shall let the mother go
But the eggs you may take for yourself." Deut. 22:6

Thank God that unlike eggs in a nest enclaved
It is not by the Law that my salvation is found;
But amazingly 'tis by Grace that I am saved,
So that God's Love may forever abound!

Casting My Mantle

1 Kings 19:19
"So Elijah departed from Horeb, and he came and found Elisha the son of Shabat, who was plowing with twelve yoke of oxen before him and Elijah passed by him and cast his mantle upon him."

There is something very prescient about this photograph,
Reminiscent of Elisha passing by while Elijah was at work;
And lest you think me to be too vain and begin to laugh,
Let me remind you this photo was taken in the Kirk!

And though young Edison was not tending his oxen
He was engaged in the labor he was given to do;
And it still holds true that God calls young men and women
To greater tasks than they have ever aspired to!

And thus it was that Elisha cast his mantle on young Elijah
Or as we would probably say in our modern translation
He tapped him on the shoulder ... as here in this replica
We see the casting of the mantle as a call to a holy vocation!

What more can I say, than that which has been said,
And which in the Old Testament we have already read;
That a young man shall stand in the old Prophets stead:
But I never dreamed that he would be a Redhead!

Elan Vital

(You cannot inhibit what you inherit)

To tell the truth, I'll be the first to admit:
"She owns me" ….and I've always known it,
Having won my adoration with her charm and wit
With which our hearts will forever be knit.

For in truth, and to be more explicit
She is the élan vital that you inhabit
For genetically you cannot inhibit
What through your mother you inherit!

This granddaughter of such angelic face
Enfolds her claim with a loving embrace;
And her "Elan Vital"** you can readily trace,
Has made me a believer in God's Evolving Grace!

** With my thanks to Henri Bergson (!859-1941)

French Philosopher (Creative Evolution / **Elan Vital**) Nobel Laureate 1927

Suffering from the Dwindles

Proverbs 13:11
"Wealth hastily gained will quickly dwindle"

My Annual Royalty Statement from my 1984 book at Chalice Press
Indicates that what I've been fearing, I now know for certain;
My income has Dwindled Down much to my financial distress
And even worse, a part of my life has seen its closing curtain!

I sense somehow that I too am suffering from the Dwindles
I now have doubts that I'll ever be published again;
For I've lost that fire in the belly that ambition kindles;
And that used to force me daily to pick up paper and pen

And I sense that my numbered days are also
Dwindling to an end;
And as time burns out the wick of my remaining birthday candles;
Now I hear the sound of 'taps' each night from distant Bugles;
And I know that I have less money as well as less time to spend.

Maybe it's true. "Wealth hastily gained will quickly dwindle"
And now seeing that I no longer will receive a Royalty Dividend.
It leaves me feeling quite disenchanted as well as quite vulnerable
Knowing that this may be an omen of my own life's end!

The Smiling Dragon that
Lives in Our Pool

"Praise the Lord you Dragons and all deeps." Psalm 148:7 KJV

The Old Testament records over 20 accounts of Dragons and
a few drawings of their frightful appearances. They were
threatening mental images which are still embedded from
childhood into the deep recesses of my mind, even to this
day. So, I chose not to subject my children to such images of

Biblical violence and instead I've filled our pool with smiling
dragons and floating toys of safety and friendliness.

The dragon and the dog shall frolic together
Mother and child shall embrace the bouncing waves;
Grandmother entices granddaughter to step in and enter
What everyone enjoys what everyone craves !

God's creation is 'Good' as God declared. (Gen. 1:31)
A balanced world to serve His purpose;
Our calling is to enjoy the dragon we once feared
And share God's world with him whereso'er he goes!

When the Cows Come Home

Psalm 104:23 *"As man goeth forth unto his
work and to his labor until evening"*

When the cows come home
At their long days end,
They rarely wander, stray or roam;
But singly and silently they slowly wend
Their way to their home up on the hill
As if they were led by God's eternal will.

What instinct draws them back each night?
What inner signal turns them homeward?
Is it some mystical and sacred bovine rite?
Or God's design in His creating Word
That causes cows to leave their meadows
And brings them home at each day's close?

The farmer's faith is to believe
That when the evening comes;
The cows will tum and slowly leave
To answer their eternal summons
Bringing them back to the place from whence
Their journey did at first commence.

When my labor on earth comes to an end
And the shadows of death begin to draw nigh;
When the clouds of evening on me descend,
I wonder if I... if I
Will hear that voice in the evening gloom,
Calling me to "Come Home, Come Home.

High Anxiety

Psalm 34:7
"The angel of the Lord watches over those who
love Him and He delivers them."

High Anxiety is that critical moment in your life
When you feel that you're at the end of your rope!
An existential moment when in human strife
You feel that an angel of God is your only hope!

I faced that moment all too regularly during the war,
As a young sailor on a Destroyer I lived in an emotional squall
Not a fear of the enemy's torpedoes or guns on shore
But the fear of hearing the Captain calling out: "Swim Call"

Jumping off the ship into the deep just to go for swim
With my fear of sharks kept me in a state of high anxiety;
My whole life lay in the hands of a testy Captain's whim
And my prayers to my guardian angels who were watching over me!

**Historical Note: In 1950, off the shore of Tanchon, Korea (after I had
been transferred to Honolulu) the U.S.S. Brush hit a mine amidships
that broke her keel. Thirteen of my former shipmates were killed and
31 injured.

Christmas Eve at the State Penitentiary

(Written while I was Chairman of the
Nebraska State Board of Parole)

Chapter 2 of the Gospel according to Saint Luke

Now in that region there were guards standing out in their towers
Keeping watch over their prisoners by night.
And searchlights round about them, shone through the long hours
Until the coming of the morning light,

And the everlasting brightness of those prison yard lights
Glistened silently off the high-strung razor wire;
And on this the holiest of all winter nights
No eye could see, no ear could hear the heavenly angel choir.

And while guards watched and waited for their shifts to end
And arc lights beamed down on the prison yard
The inmates were all locked down to spend
A sleepless night on beds both bare and hard;
Lined up in numbered rows and tiers
To serve unnumbered days and years
In lonely cells, where fear dispels
Any hope of peace, or early release.

And on that night in human history
In what we call the incarnation
As God revealed his love in that manger mystery
Which is the joy of our Christmas celebration;
The star of Bethlehem made no penetration
Upon the inmates in that prison population;
For the Star that night could not be seen
For all were blinded by the brightness of the searchlight's beam.

I sense that we too, often need to be reminded
Of the coming of the true light of God's incarnate word;
For we too are often likewise blinded;
By the bright lights of our secular world!

The 'Ritual of Friendship' in the Bulletin

Rulers of the earth, and all peoples, young
and old, men and women together,
God has raised up a horn of safety for us all.
Praise the Lord!

★"How Great Thou Art". # 467   OSTOREGUD

WELCOME *(Please pass the Ritual of Friendship pad.)*
          The Lord by with you.
     And also with you.

                    ★Those who are able, please stand.

It's about that line in the bulletin ... written in italics
Indicating it's time to observe the "Ritual of Friendship"
An error like this is what makes modern agnostics
Laugh in derision at our attempts at Discipleship!

It's a contradiction in terms, as you certainly must see,
For if it's a ritual then it is certainly not friendship:
For a ritual is a 'rite'…something of a formal ceremony
Which has nothing to do with koinonia or kinship!

Friendship, by definition is not a means to an end
But rather a relationship to which you are irresistibly drawn.
Sharing empathy and trust are the gifts of a friend
Not something you pass down the aisle or casually spawn!!!

Why don't we call it "A Moment of Greeting?"
A cacophony of casual salutations and salaams;
Admit that our "Ritual" is inherently self-defeating
And clean up our worship from all these phony shams!'

'Twas just a thought ….

A prayer for our newly elected Pastor Nominating Committee

BY DON MCCALL

May your first thought be like the last thought
Expressed in the movie Casablanca's final quip;
When Claude Rains says to Bogart at the airport
"I think this is the beginning of a beautiful friendship"

So I pray, not for a great preacher, priest or saint
I'd be happy and would welcome without any complaint
A Pastor who would prove to be a friend for us
A Friend ... like the "Friend we have in Jesus"

Recently our Pastor retired and our church was faced with the task of selecting a new pastor.

It so happened that my wife was selected to serve on that committee. I was happy for her because I knew that it would be an exciting and worthwhile experience and that as a lawyer she would be a good addition to the committee.

On the Sunday the nominated members were duly elected by

the congregation they were invited to come forward, to the front of the sanctuary, where they accepted the congregation's vote of their election. Then the minister pronounced the Benediction and the service was over.

I mentioned on the way home that I rather wished that there had been a prayer for the PNC included in the body of the worship service. I told Barb that if there was any body that needed the prayers of the congregation it would be the PNC. When I got home, I decided to write a prayer for them...just of my own frustration!

Then I sent a copy to the Presbyterian Outlook Magazine. They in turn decided to publish my letter and it arrived in magazine form on the very weekend the PNC was interviewing the last candidate. He accepted the Call. I had to pause for a moment to wonder whether it was Providence or Coincidence that brought about our good fortune....but in my heart, I believe I know!

At The Helm

*"Therefore, since we are surrounded by so great
a cloud of witnesses..." Hebrews 12:1*

This is wee Ian, my youngest Grandson at the helm
Steering my sailboat on the course of his own choosing;
His eyes on the horizon as if the whole world were his realm
And daring to determine the course we'd be cruising!

Little did he sense that his Uncle was also holding the wheel
With strength to override any wrong course that Ian might set;
Nor did he know…nor was he aware …nor could he feel
That his father had a firm grip on the back of his life jacket!

Theologically, this is what we call God's prevenient Grace,
Which surrounds us by a great cloud of angels in our travels;
Who lovingly hovers over us, while we at our own pace,
March boldly through life as our destiny unravels!

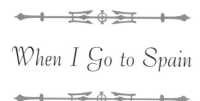

When I Go to Spain

"I hope to see you in passing when I go to Spain." Romans 15:24

In the Apostle Paul's letter to the church at Rome
He makes his future plans quite plain;
By announcing that the next time he leaves home
His hope and dream is to set sail for Spain!

For Paul the evangelist, could not rest
Until he'd taken the Gospel of Good News;
From Jerusalem in the East to Spain in the West
As the Word of God for both gentiles and Jews!

But Paul's never saw his dream come true
He never took the voyage planned and intended;
But as he teaches us in Romans 15:22
Our dreams are often providentially amended!

The owner of this sailboat, I would guess
Also had dreams of sailing some uncharted sea;
But it appears his work somehow failed to progress
And now her hull lies unfinished, tarnished and rusty.

Yet still she stands there, the dream of his soul
Cradled on dry land where everyone can see;
His efforts to fulfill his lifetime goal
His dream of someday going to sea!

Some dreams I guess will always go unfulfilled
Some sails I'm sure will never be unfurled;
But ours is still to do what God has willed
In whatever we do in His world.

A Lesson Learned Early in Life

I Corinthians 12:15-26 (excerpts)

Indeed, the body does not consist of one member but of many. If the foot would say to the hand, because I am not a hand, that does not make the foot any less a part of the body. And if the ear would say that because I am not an eye, I do not belong to the body that would not make it any less a part of the body. As it is, there are many members yet the body is one. Thus there may be no dissention, but that the members may have the same care for one another. If one member suffers, all suffer together with it; if one member is honored, all rejoice together with him.

This is my grade school soccer team in Lebanon
I'm in the first row: Brother Bill is holding the ball;
This picture was taken right after we had won
A game that really wasn't consequential at all.

What was important was that we had played together,
Each one of us had contributed to the whole.
And what we enjoyed the most, we'll always remember
Was that our 'Friendship' was really our primary goal!

Note: Mounir (in the front row with me) is still one of my closest friends who has visited me in Rochester and whom I have visited in Brasilia. We play tennis each time we meet, agreeing that the host will be the winning player.

My Quiver Is Full

"Children are a heritage from the Lord. Blessed is the man
Whose quiver is full of them." Psalm 127:3-5

My Dad's life inspired us all ...
in fact, it almost overwhelmed us:
Presbyterian Missionary Headmaster of a Lebanese academy,
Wartime member of General Donovan's OSS Corps 'Invictus',
And then PhD College Professor, as a final plus.
More than that
He was devoted to his family and his ordination vows.

To his golfing Scottish Heritage and enjoying the game
As well as tennis and all else that family time allows.
But mostly just going sailing and being the heritage we all claim.
But frankly
We loved him the most just for his being with us
Not what he did or said compared with moments ever so wondrous;
For we remember a love ever so bountiful
Carried in his quiver ever so full.

A Fist Bump Benediction

Luke Chapter 2

I Love old First Church!
And all the memories of her that I carry in my heart.
But there is one memory I enjoy which is mine alone:
'Twas a Christmas Eve service now forever set apart
From any other that I've ever experienced or known.

It was a Christmas Eve
And the church was packed with all the born again:
The transept balconies which lie crosswise to the nave,
Held families with an abundance of squiggly children
Whom I knew wouldn't be able to be quiet or behave.

But it was Christmas
Therefore, my homilies were as brief as time would permit
Brief but poignant reminders of that birth in Bethlehem;
For the Benediction, (because of the crowd) I remained in the pulpit
Where I raised my hand to offer a Christmas blessing and an Amen.

I could sense how Jesus must have felt when surrounded by a crowd.
Touching back then, even as now, was not always allowed.
Then I sensed a small hand reaching down to touch me
When I looked up I saw a small boy in the balcony.

And then he gave me a thumbs up 'fist bump'
And an angel from heaven whispered in my ear:
"…… and a little child shall lead them"

From the South Side of Mt. Sinai

(What do you do when your face no longer shines?)

Exodus 34:29
"When Moses came down from the mountain, he did not know that
the skin from his face shone because he had been talking to God."

I spent several days here at St. Catherine's Monastery
Nestled in the Sinai desert at the base of the Holy Mountain;
Sharing in the monk's life of study, prayer and spirituality
All to prepare myself for a sense of the Holy that I might attain.

I ascended the mountain at night under a full moon
Wanting to be near the top to see the sunrise;
The path was well worn: The mighty rocks were well hewn,
Each step upward toward God was a glorious surprise.

I remember that when Moses descended from that moment of wonder
His face was shining in the resplendence of his meeting the Almighty;
Thereafter, Moses always wore a facial veil as proof of that encounter,
And I quietly wished that the same transformation would come over me.

What surprised me the most when I descended from the mountain
Was not that my face wasn't shining, an acknowledged factual detail;
But that I no longer felt the need to publically
prove my encounter by wearing a veil,
My transformation was that I felt no need
to have a veil of pretense prevail.

Scripture tells us that as time passed, the shining of Moses' face diminished. However, he continued to wear the veil to keep the people from noticing that his glory was fading. The Apostle Paul states that in an encounter with Christ there is no need for a veil. *"When one turns to the Lord, the veil is removed. And all of us with unveiled faces are being transformed."2 Corinthians 3:18*

My Life's Greatest Fear

*"I say unto you that in that very night, two will be in
one bed; one will be taken, and the other left"*
Luke 17:34

I awoke this morning with an ominous sense of dread
As if a bad dream hadn't ended upon my waking;
I rolled over and reached out for you across the bed
Wanting some assurance that would calm my quaking...

Instantly I knew that something was terribly wrong
The sheets were warm and rumpled but you were gone;
My sense of alarm then grew exceedingly strong
And I was stricken by a sense of feeling totally woebegone.

My greatest fear these days as my life draws to an end
Is not the fear of the loss of my health or my wealth
But rather the fear of your dying first; and my having to spend
The rest of my days all alone grieving over your death!

I assure you that it's not just my competitive nature
That makes me want to be the first to be taken;
For the one thing in this life that I know for sure
Is that I don't want to live alone.... loveless and forsaken!

That's why I was so happy to see you in the family room
Reading the paper and enjoying your morning coffee.
But next time don't leave me sleeping alone in a deep sense of doom
Instead give me a lingering kiss and let your love waken me!

For my greatest fear in life is not death itself
But rather living after you have already passed on;
I don't want to be left sitting like leftovers on the shelf
I'd much rather be the first one to be gone!

So Lord, I pray, help me overcome My Greatest Fear
Namely, that "If two will be in one bed"
Please, Lord, let me now volunteer
To be the one to go on ahead!

The End

(To Barbara)

If you've read in the papers of my premature demise
It's probably just another one of those journalistic lies;
    Or if you read that I died 'peaceably in the night'
    It's probably just another fact they didn't get right;

The truth is that after your loving good night kiss
I realized that I would be totally restless and remiss
    If I didn't somehow endeavor to once again seek
    A quick 'curtain call' or at least a peck on the cheek

All the while thinking that before I became a heavenly guest,
    There to abide in my well-earned heavenly rest
    I'd first gladly die for another one of your kisses
        And I did.
        Amen.